Amazing Animals
Zebras

Please visit our web site at www.garethstevens.com
For a free catalog describing our list of high-quality books, call 1-800-542-2595 (USA) or 1-800-387-3178 (Canada). Our fax: 1-877-542-2596

Library of Congress Cataloging-in-Publication Data

Wilsdon, Christina.
    Zebras / by Christina Wilsdon.—U.S. ed.
          p. cm.—(Amazing Animals)
        Originally published: Pleasantville, NY: Reader's Digest Young Familiies, c2005.
        Includes bibliographical references and index.
        ISBN-10: 0-8368-9113-9 ISBN-13: 978-0-8368-9113-3 (lib. bdg.)
        ISBN-10: 1-4339-2030-1 ISBN-13: 978-1-4339-2030-1 (soft cover)
    1. Zebras—Juvenile literature. I. Title.
    QL737.U62W57 2009
    599.665'7—dc22   2008027912

This edition first published in 2009 by
Gareth Stevens Publishing
A Weekly Reader® Company
1 Reader's Digest Road
Pleasantville, NY 10570-7000 USA

This edition copyright © 2009 by Gareth Stevens, Inc. Original edition copyright © 2005 by Reader's Digest Young Families, Pleasantville, NY 10570

Gareth Stevens Senior Managing Editor: Lisa M. Herrington
Gareth Stevens Creative Director: Lisa Donovan
Gareth Stevens Art Director: Ken Crossland
Gareth Stevens Associate Editor: Amanda Hudson
Gareth Stevens Publisher: Keith Garton

Consultant: Robert E. Budliger (Retired), NY State Department of Environmental Conservation

Photo Credits
Front cover: Dynamic Graphics, Inc. title page: image 100 ltd. Contents: Digital Vision. pages 6-7: Corbis Corporation. page 8-9: IT Stock. page 10 (bottom): Nova Development Corporation. pages 10-11: IT Stock. pages 12-13: John Foxx Images. pages 14-15: Photodisc by Getty Images. pages 16-17: Digital Vision. page 17 (bottom right): Nova Development Corporation. page 18 (lower left): Nova Development Corporation. pages 18-19: Photodisc by Getty Images. pages 20-21: Brand X Pictures. pages 22-23: PhotoDisc. pages 24-25: Brand X Pictures. page 26 (bottom): Nova Development Corporation. pages 26-27: Photodisc by Getty Images. pages 28-29: Digital Vision. pages 30-31: Dynamic Graphics, Inc. pages 32-33: Photodisc by Getty Images. page 34 (bottom): Nova Development Corporation. pages 34-35: Photodisc by Getty Images. pages 36-37: Photodisc by Getty Images. page 37 (bottom right): John Foxx Images. pages 38-39: PhotoDisc. page 41 (bottom right): Brand X Pictures. page 43: PhotoDisc. pages 44-45: Brand X Pictures. Back cover: Brand X Pictures.

Printed in the United States of America

1 2 3 4 5 6 7 8 9 13 12 11 10 09

Amazing Animals
Zebras

By Christina Wilsdon

 Gareth Stevens
Publishing

Contents

Chapter 1
A Zebra Story

Mane Event

A baby zebra's **mane** runs all the way down its back—from its ears to its tail! The little zebra loses most of the mane on its back when it is a few weeks old.

A herd of zebras **graze** on an African grassland. Their tails swish, flicking away flies. The zebras look up as one female walks away from the group. Then they drop their heads and keep grazing.

The father zebra, however, follows the mother zebra. She is about to give birth. It is his job to stand guard nearby.

Carefully, the mother lies down. Her baby is born quickly. The mother jumps to her feet, then nuzzles her baby. The mother licks him with her big tongue.

Ten minutes later, the baby, too, is on his feet. He sways on his long, skinny legs. Just half an hour later, he is able to walk—and fifteen minutes after that, he can run! Now he can flee with his mother if a hungry lion chases them.

Wild Words

A baby zebra is called a **foal**. (The word foal rhymes with the word goal.)

9

The mother zebra leads her baby back to the group. She shields him from the other zebras, kicking and nipping any that come near. She will not let her baby get to know the other zebras for a few days. First he must learn that she is his mother.

A week passes. The baby grows plump from drinking his mother's rich milk. Sometimes he nibbles on grass, but milk is his main food until he is six months old.

The baby zebra stays close to his mother, but as he gets older, he leaves her side now and then to play with other foals. They love to chase each other. They even chase birds and other animals!

Baby Stripes

Baby zebras often have brown and white stripes when they are born. They are fuzzier than their mothers.

By his first birthday, the baby zebra has become a big, strong **colt**. He can take care of himself. But he still follows his mother, who has just given birth to a new baby.

Some colts stay with their family group until they are four years old. But one day, the colt's brothers leave to form a small group of their own. He dashes off with them, kicking and play-fighting as they go.

The **mare's** new baby is a female—a **filly**. She will stay with her family until she is about one and a half years old. Then she will go off to join another **stallion's** herd of mares, spending the rest of her life with them.

All Grown Up

A filly usually has her first baby when she is about two and a half years old. A colt does not become a stallion with his own herd until he is about six years old.

Chapter 2
The Body of a Zebra

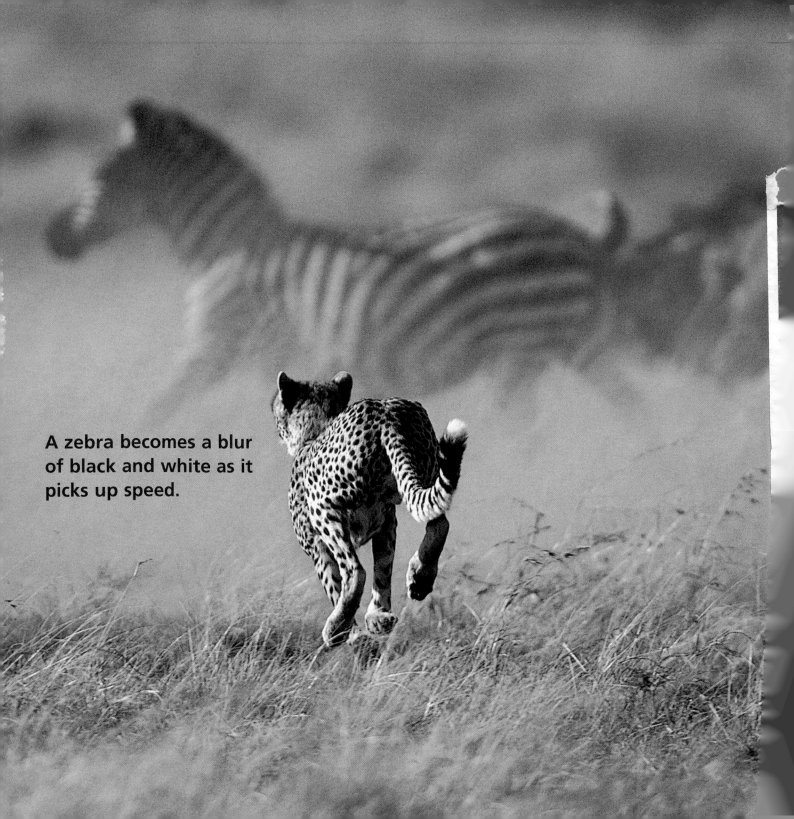

A zebra becomes a blur of black and white as it picks up speed.

Racing Stripes

Zebras are wild cousins of horses and donkeys. The most common kind of zebra—the **plains** zebra—is about the size of a big pony. A stiff mane sticks up from its neck like bristles on a brush. Wide stripes march down its neck and body and loop around its rump.

Like horses, zebras depend on speed to escape **predators**. A zebra can gallop at nearly 40 miles (64 kilometers) per hour. Big muscles bunched up at the top of its legs give the zebra its power. Strong fibers in its legs stretch, helping the zebra spring forward.

A zebra can flare its nostrils wide to gulp down air, and a big chest helps it take deep breaths as it runs. The extra oxygen helps the zebra run faster.

Shoo, Fly!

A zebra's tail is 20 inches (51 centimeters) long. It makes an excellent flyswatter! A zebra can also twitch its skin to shake off flies.

Alert for Danger

Zebras are a favorite meal of lions, leopards, hyenas, cheetahs, and wild hunting dogs. Zebras watch carefully for these predators.

The location of the zebra's eyes help the zebra to spot danger. The eyes sit on the sides of its head, which allows the zebra to see behind it and in front of it. The eyes are also placed high up, so the zebra can see even when its nose is deep in a patch of grass.

If a zebra spies a lion, it snorts loudly. It may turn and face the lion and even stamp its hoof. Other zebras may join in. Then the lion knows that the game is over. It has lost its chance to launch a surprise attack!

Beautiful Dreamer

Like all animals, zebras need to sleep. One zebra stands guard while others rest. This zebra's half-shut eyes show that it is taking a nap. A zebra can doze while standing because its legs lock in place to hold it up. At night, zebras may lie flat on their sides to sleep.

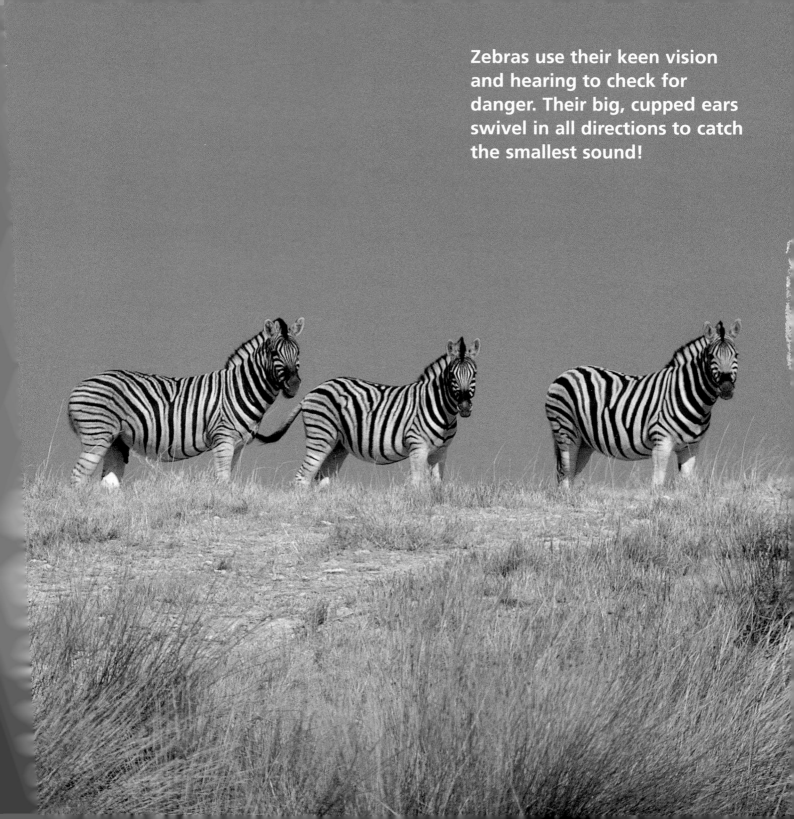

Zebras use their keen vision and hearing to check for danger. Their big, cupped ears swivel in all directions to catch the smallest sound!

Each zebra has its own voice. Other zebras in its family can recognize it by sound alone!

That's a Mouthful!

Grass is hard to eat. It is stringy and tough. But a zebra's teeth are up to the job. A zebra gathers grass with its long, rubbery lips. Then it grabs the blades with strong, curved teeth at the front of its mouth. With a jerk of its head, it rips off the grass tips. Its big tongue shovels the grass deeper into its mouth. Finally, the broad teeth in the back crush the grass. Ridges on the teeth grind it into pulp. The zebra's jaws go around and around as it chews.

Chewing grass wears down teeth. A zebra's teeth, however, are long and deeply set in its jaws. They slowly push up and out from the gums so that the zebra is able to continue chewing throughout its life.

Sounding Off

Zebras don't neigh like horses, but they are noisy! A plains zebra calls to other zebras with a loud barking, whistling bray. Baby zebras squeal. Fighting zebras squeal and grunt. A relaxed zebra blows air out of its nose and mouth with a fluttering sound just like a horse.

Wild Words

When zebras **bray**, they make sounds similar to those made by donkeys.

Chapter 3

Zebra Stripes

23

Take a close look at the three plains zebras in this picture. Can you see how their stripes differ? Each zebra has its own special pattern of stripes. No two zebras are exactly alike!

Stripes Galore!

The first thing we notice about a zebra are its stripes. No other animal, not even its close cousin the horse, looks like a zebra. Its bold pattern led to its nickname, "tiger-horse."

At first glance, zebra stripes look alike. But there is a huge variety of stripes. Plains zebras have big, bold stripes. Other kinds of zebras have thinner stripes—and more of them. The thinnest stripes belong to the Grevy's zebra. It has more than twice as many stripes on its body than a plains zebra. Some Grevy's zebras have reddish brown stripes. Mountain zebras have thinner stripes than plains zebras, but they have thicker stripes than Grevy's zebras.

Tail End

Each kind of zebra looks different from the back. The stripes on a Grevy's zebra whirl in circles around its tail. A patch of white surrounds the wide black stripe on its back. A plains zebra has stripes ending in triangles pointing at its tail.

Grevy's zebra

Plains zebra

Strange Stripes

Some rare zebras are striped in reverse! They are black where they should be white, and white where they should be black. They look like black horses with thin white stripes. Some zebras' stripes blend together so that they look black with white spots. An albino zebra has no black at all. It is white with beige stripes.

Striped Clues

A zebra's stripes are a clue to where it lives. A zebra of the northern plains has black and white stripes. Its legs are striped all the way down to its hooves. A zebra from the south has dark stripes, but they are not pitch-black. They may even be brown. The lower parts of its legs are white, not striped.

Shadow Stripes

Some zebras of the southern plains have pale stripes in the white spaces between black stripes. These are called shadow stripes. They can be seen on this zebra mare's rump and sides. Her foal has shadow stripes, too.

Even a zebra's mane is striped. The stripes on the neck of this Grevy's zebra reach up into its mane. A mane helps protect a zebra's neck from bites by other zebras.

Stripes may help protect zebras. When zebras race across the plains, their stripes become blurry. This makes it difficult for a predator to focus on just one zebra.

Why Do Zebras Have Stripes?

Some scientists think stripes help zebras escape predators. A herd of zebras looks like a blur when it runs. This might confuse a predator. But lions do not seem to be confused by stripes.

Stripes do break up the shape of a zebra. It is easier to see a dark body from far away than a zebra's striped body. But that is only if the zebra is standing still—and zebras do not freeze when they see a lion!

Stripes may help keep zebra families together. Zebras recognize their family members' stripes. However, horses have no problem recognizing other horses. Why should zebras need them?

Stripes may help ward off insects. Scientists have found that some insects would rather land on dark animal skin than light or striped skin. But zebras still get bitten by other insects.

So why do zebras have stripes? We may never be sure!

Chapter 4
Zebra Herds

One zebra stands guard as the others drink at a water hole. All the zebras have their ears pricked to listen for danger. Lions may be hiding nearby, and crocodiles may be lurking underwater.

Families Together

Huge herds of zebras graze on the African plains. In the wet season, they stay in one place to eat fresh grass. In the dry season, hundreds of zebras trek across the land to find food and water.

These big herds are made up of many small families. Each family includes a stallion (the male), a few mares (the females), and their foals (baby or young zebras). Foals in one family play with foals from other families, but the mares do not mix. Mares in different families will snap at one another if they get too close. Stallions greet other stallions by sniffing noses, then rearing and jumping away.

Why do all these families herd together? Because there is safety in numbers. Many pairs of eyes looking for danger help all the zebras stay alive. When predators do attack, it's safer to be part of a thundering herd!

Neighbor-Herds

Zebras often form large herds with other kinds of animals. **Wildebeest**, gazelles, and giraffes are common companions. Warthogs, elephants, and even ostriches may be part of the herd, too. Herding together helps all the animals—it means more eyes, ears, and noses on the alert!

Zebras, wildebeest, and gazelles all eat grass, but they do not compete for food, because each one grazes differently. Zebras eat the top parts of grass blades. Wildebeest graze on shorter grass. The little gazelles nibble on new grass.

All Aboard!

Oxpecker birds often ride on zebras' backs. Sometimes a zebra may carry more than a dozen of them—and even have birds hanging off its sides and belly! Zebras have a deal with oxpeckers. The birds clean pesky bugs off the zebra's skin and get a meal at the same time. A zebra knows a predator is near when the birds hiss and fly away.

oxpecker

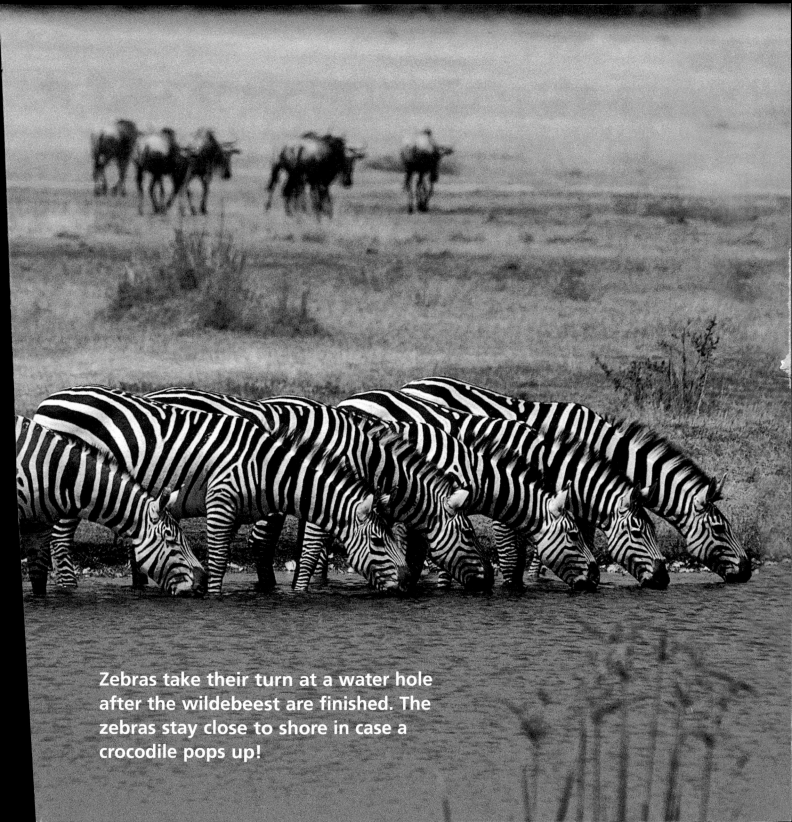

Zebras take their turn at a water hole after the wildebeest are finished. The zebras stay close to shore in case a crocodile pops up!

Each mare in a herd has her own place in line. Young zebras walk behind their mothers. If a mare tries to cut in front of another zebra, the other mares kick and bite her until she goes back to her place!

Getting Along

The stallion is the leader of a zebra family. He chases other stallions away from his mares and foals. A stallion also protects his family from predators. He runs in between his family and a predator and also stands behind them at water holes.

One mare helps the stallion manage the family. She is often the oldest mare. She always walks in front of the other mares to lead them on trails, with the stallion last in line.

The mares in a family form close bonds with one another. They stay together as a family even if the stallion dies and a new stallion takes over.

You Scratch My Back, I'll Scratch Yours

Zebras spend hours **grooming** themselves and one another. Two zebras often stand side by side, head to tail. Each zebra grooms the other's neck and back. This helps zebras clean parts that are hard to reach. By facing opposite ways, they can also watch out for danger in all directions.

Chapter 5
Zebras in the World

Where Zebras Live

ARCTIC OCEAN

NORTH AMERICA

EUROPE

ASIA

PACIFIC OCEAN

ATLANTIC OCEAN

PACIFIC OCEAN

AFRICA

SOUTH AMERICA

INDIAN OCEAN

AUSTRALIA

The **purple** area shows where plains zebras live.

The **green** areas show where mountain zebras live.

The **brown** area shows where Grevy's zebras live.

Zebras of the Past

Just over 100 years ago, there lived a kind of zebra called the "quagga." Quaggas sported red-brown stripes on their heads, necks, and shoulders. They had red-brown bodies and white legs. But by the late 1800s, they were extinct. Europeans had hunted them for their hides and had taken over their grasslands so that cattle could feed there instead. Laws now protect zebras.

Zebra Habitats

There are three main types of zebras. They live in different **habitats** in Africa.

The most common type is the plains zebra that lives on the plains and the **savanna**. A savanna is a grassland that has trees. Plains zebras range from southwestern to eastern Africa.

The Grevy's zebra lives in dry grasslands and deserts. It can be found in parts of Kenya and Ethiopia in eastern Africa. Grevy's zebras live alone or in small groups.

Mountain zebras live in hilly parts of northeastern Africa. These little zebras have hearts that weigh more than plains zebras'. Extra powerful hearts help pump blood at high altitudes where there is less oxygen in the air.

Zebras Big and Small

Of the three types of zebras, the smallest is the mountain zebra. It is about 4 feet (1.2 meters) high at the shoulder. The biggest is the Grevy's zebra, shown here. It can be as big as a full-grown horse.

The Future of Zebras

Today the plains zebra is not in danger of extinction. But two other kinds of zebra—the Grevy's zebra and the mountain zebra—are **endangered**. Fortunately, zebras are now protected by law from hunters. And some lands have been set aside as **preserves** for zebras and other animals.

But big cattle herds still compete with zebras for food and water. Farmers also drain water from rivers for crops. Scientists and other people are working with Africa's farmers and herders to help protect zebras and their habitat.

Fast Facts About Plains Zebras

Scientific name	*Equus burchelli*
Class	Mammalia
Order	Perissodactyla
Size	4 to 5 feet (1.2 to 1.5 m) tall at shoulders
Weight	Males up to 900 pounds (408 kg); Females up to 500 pounds (227 kg)
Lifespan	About 18 years in the wild About 30 years in captivity
Habitat	Grasslands and savannas
Top speed	About 40 miles (64 km) per hour

Glossary

bray — to make loud sounds like those of a donkey

colt — a young male zebra

endangered — a species of animal or plant in danger of extinction

filly — a young female zebra

foal — a baby zebra

graze — to eat grass

grooming — cleaning of fur, skin, or feathers by an animal

habitat — the natural environment where an animal or plant lives

mane — hair growing along the back of an animal's neck

mare — an adult female zebra

plain — a large, flat area of dry land; a grassland

predator — an animal that hunts and eats other animals to survive

preserves — areas of land or water where wildlife and plants are protected

savanna — a flat grassland with trees in a warm area of the world

stallion — an adult male zebra

wildebeest — another word for a gnu, an antelope that looks a bit like an ox with big, curved horns

Zebras: Show What You Know

How much have you learned about zebras? Grab a piece of paper and a pencil and write your answers down.

1. What is another name for a baby zebra?

2. At about what age does a female zebra usually have her first baby?

3. Which type of zebra has the thinnest stripes?

4. How might a zebra's stripes help keep it together with its family?

5. How does herding together with different kinds of animals help to keep zebras safe?

6. What type of bird often rides on the backs of zebras?

7. Why do zebras stay close to the shore at water holes?

8. Which relative of the zebra is now extinct?

9. What are the three main types of zebras?

10. Which type of zebra is the smallest?

1. Foal 2. Two and a half years old 3. The Grevy's zebra 4. Zebras can recognize the stripes of family members. 5. More eyes, ears, and noses on the alert for predators! 6. Oxpecker bird 7. So they can watch out for crocodiles. 8. The quagga 9. Plains zebra, Grevy's zebra, mountain zebra 10. The mountain zebra

For More Information

Books

Little Zebras. Born to be Wild (series). Guidoux, Valerie. (Gareth Stevens, 2005)

Zebras. Nature Watch (series). Stone, Lynn. (Lerner Publications, 2008)

Zebras. Wild Ones (series). Anderson, Jill. (NorthWord Books for Young Readers, 2005)

Web Sites

African Wildlife Foundation

www.awf.org/content/wildlife/detail/zebra

Learn all sorts of facts about zebras, and find out how you can help protect their habitats. Be sure to check out the video clips from Serengeti National Park in Africa.

San Diego Zoo: Zebras

www.sandiegozoo.org/animalbytes/t-zebra.html

Check out this site for fun facts, photos, and information about wildlife "adoption" programs.

Publisher's note to educators and parents: Our editors have carefully reviewed these web sites to ensure that they are suitable for children. Many web sites change frequently, however, and we cannot guarantee that a site's future contents will continue to meet our high standards of quality and educational value. Be advised that children should be closely supervised whenever they access the Internet.

Index